SUSAN PIERRE-LOUIS

Winning Strategies for Life: The Athlete's Guide to Thriving in the Workplace

Utilize your sports skills for career success

First edition

This book was professionally typeset on Reedsy.
Find out more at reedsy.com

To my son, Matthew,

The athlete within you has always inspired me with your unwavering dedication, sportsmanship, and pursuit of excellence. Your passion for both the game and your studies has been a constant source of motivation, reminding me that winning strategies transcend the court and impact every aspect of life. May you continue to learn, grow, and achieve remarkable things, both on and off the court.

Contents

III   Achieving Peak Performance: Maintaining Your Competitive Edge

I

The Athlete's Mindset: Building a Foundation for Success

1

Introduction

Remember those early mornings spent practicing, the sting of defeat, and the rush of victory? Whether you were the star player or the dedicated team member, sports taught you more than just athletic skills. It built within you a unique set of tools, a winning mindset, and a spirit of camaraderie that extends far beyond the playing field.

This book, Winning Strategies for Life: The Athlete's Guide to Thriving in the Workplace, invites you to tap into that inner athlete, regardless of your experience on the field or court. We believe that the skills you honed in sports, from teamwork and communication to discipline and perseverance, are invaluable assets in the workplace.

Here's why you should read this book:

- You don't need to be a professional athlete to benefit. The lessons within are universal and applicable to anyone seeking to elevate their career.
- Unlock your potential. Learn how to apply the same winning strategies athletes use to achieve their goals and reach your full

potential in the workplace.

- Gain a competitive edge. Discover the secrets to building a resilient mindset, collaborating effectively, and navigating the challenges of the professional world.
- Develop essential skills. Master communication, time management, and leadership, empowering you to thrive in any career path you choose.
- Find your tribe. Connect with a community of individuals who share your passion and commitment to achieving success.

Winning Strategies for Life: The Athlete's Guide to Thriving in the Workplace is not just a book; it's a guide to unlocking your inner champion. It's about harnessing the power of your athletic experience, regardless of how extensive it may be, and transforming it into a springboard for career success.

So, whether you're a recent graduate, a seasoned professional seeking a change, or simply someone who wants to unlock their full potential, this book is for you. Let's step into Winning Strategies for Life: The Athlete's Guide to Thriving in the Workplace and embark on a journey of self-discovery and career achievement. Together, we will unlock the secrets of winning and build a foundation for a brighter, more successful future.

2

The Power of Positive Thinking: Cultivating Optimism and Resilience for Workplace Success

From the field or court to the boardroom, one of the most significant differentiators between high performers and average achievers is their mindset. While talent and skill are crucial, it's the unwavering belief in oneself and the ability to bounce back from setbacks that truly propel individuals toward success. This chapter delves into the power of positive thinking, exploring how athletes cultivate optimism and resilience, and how these traits can translate to achieve significant results in the workplace.

Harnessing the Power of Optimism:

Athletes are trained to see the glass as half full, focusing on possibilities rather than obstacles. This optimistic outlook fosters a sense of confidence, motivation, and determination. When faced with a challenging opponent or a seemingly insurmountable obstacle, athletes believe they can overcome it. This positive self-belief fuels their perseverance and ultimately leads to success.

In the workplace, cultivating optimism is equally important. When faced with a difficult project, a tight deadline, or a critical review, a positive attitude can make a world of difference. Optimistic individuals are more likely to see challenges as opportunities for growth and learning. They are more resilient in the face of setbacks and are more likely to find solutions and achieve their goals.

Building Resilience: The Bounce-Back Factor:

In the world of sports, setbacks and disappointments are inevitable. Injuries, losses, and missed opportunities are all part of the game. However, what separates successful athletes from those who struggle is their ability to bounce back from adversity. They possess remarkable resilience and the mental toughness to overcome challenges and setbacks. They don't let failures define them; instead, they use them as fuel to propel them forward.

Similarly, in the workplace, there will be times when things don't go as planned. Projects may fail, deadlines may be missed, and performance reviews may not be as positive as hoped. However, individuals who possess resilience will not be deterred by these setbacks. They will pick themselves up, learn from their mistakes, and move forward with renewed determination.

Developing a Positive Mindset:

The good news is that positive thinking and resilience can be cultivated. Here are some strategies that athletes use to develop these valuable mental attributes:

- Focus on the positive: Train your mind to focus on the positive aspects of a situation, even when faced with challenges.
- Set realistic goals: Setting achievable goals and celebrating your successes will boost your confidence and motivation.
- Visualize success: Athletes often visualize themselves performing at their best before a competition. This helps them stay focused and confident.
- Practice positive self-talk: Replace negative self-talk with positive affirmations and encouragement.
- Develop a support network: Surround yourself with positive and supportive people who believe in you.
- Learn from mistakes: Don't dwell on your mistakes, instead, learn from them and use them as opportunities for growth.
- Practice gratitude: Taking time to appreciate the good things in your life can help you maintain a positive outlook.

Unlocking Your Potential:

By adopting the strategies used by athletes to cultivate optimism and resilience, you can unlock your full potential and achieve greater success in the workplace. Remember, success is not a straight line. There will be bumps and detours along the way. However, by maintaining a positive attitude and bouncing back from setbacks, you can overcome any obstacle and achieve your career goals.

Actionable Tips:

- Start each day with a positive affirmation.
- Visualize yourself achieving your goals.
- Surround yourself with positive people.
- Practice gratitude daily.

- Learn from your mistakes and move forward.
- Celebrate your successes, no matter how small.

By incorporating these simple tips into your daily routine, you can cultivate a positive mindset and develop the resilience needed to thrive in the workplace and achieve your career aspirations.

3

From Playbook to Project Plan: Setting Goals and Achieving Objectives

Just like athletes meticulously plan their training and approach each game with a clear objective, achieving success in your career requires a similar focus on setting and achieving goals. In this chapter, we'll delve into the goal-setting strategies of successful athletes and demonstrate how these principles can be applied to your career development, transforming you from a casual participant to a champion in the professional arena.

The Athlete's Approach to Goal Setting:

- Specificity and Measurability: Athletes set specific, measurable, achievable, relevant, and time-bound (SMART) goals. They don't simply aim for "improvement" or "success"; they quantify their desires, setting clear benchmarks for progress and achievement. For example, an athlete might aim to run a 5K race in 20 minutes or increase their batting average by 10%.
- Visualization: Athletes visualize their success, mentally rehearsing their performance and achieving their goals. This mental rehearsal

boosts confidence and focus, preparing them for the challenges ahead.

- Breaking Down the Big Picture: Achieving large goals often feels overwhelming. Athletes master the art of breaking down their goals into smaller, actionable steps. This creates a roadmap to success, allowing them to focus on the present moment and celebrate incremental achievements.
- Continuous Assessment and Adjustment: Athletes consistently analyze their performance, identifying areas for improvement and adjusting their strategies accordingly. This agile approach ensures they stay on track and adapt to changing circumstances.

Applying Athletic Goal Setting to Your Career:

- Identify Your Career Aspirations: What do you want to achieve in your career? Be specific and define your goals in concrete terms. Do you want to land a specific role, acquire a new skill, or launch your own business?
- Set SMART Goals: Translate your career aspirations into SMART goals. This provides a clear roadmap for your journey and empowers you to measure your progress along the way.
- Break Down Your Goals: Divide your large goals into manageable milestones and smaller, actionable steps. This makes progress feel tangible and helps you stay motivated throughout the process.
- Develop a Plan of Action: Create a detailed plan outlining the specific steps you will take to achieve your goals. Include timelines, resources needed, and potential challenges you may face.
- Celebrate Milestones and Adapt: Take the time to celebrate your accomplishments, no matter how small. Recognizing your progress will boost your confidence and motivation. Continuously assess your performance and adjust your plan as needed to stay on track.

Actionable Tips for Success:

- Write down your goals: This increases your commitment and makes them more concrete.
- Share your goals with trusted mentors or colleagues: This fosters accountability and encourages support.
- Visualize your success: Take time to imagine yourself achieving your goals.
- Develop a daily routine: This helps you stay focused and productive.
- Seek out feedback and guidance: Don't be afraid to ask for help when you need it.

By adopting the goal-setting strategies of athletes, you can transform your career aspirations into tangible achievements. Remember, success is not a destination; it's a journey filled with challenges and triumphs. By applying the same focus and determination that athletes demonstrate on the field, you can overcome any obstacle and achieve your full potential in the workplace. So, set your sights high, embrace the challenge, and unleash your inner champion.

4

Building Mental Toughness: From Athlete to Professional Champion

In the competitive world of sports, mental strength can be the deciding factor between victory and defeat. Athletes cultivate a powerful inner resilience, enabling them to overcome pressure, adversity, and setbacks. This same mental toughness is equally crucial for success in the professional arena. In this chapter, we'll explore how athletes develop mental fortitude and translate these strategies to equip you with the tools to conquer challenges and emerge stronger from setbacks in your career.

The Pillars of Mental Toughness:

- Resilience: The ability to bounce back from setbacks, learn from mistakes, and persevere in the face of adversity is paramount for both athletes and professionals. Athletes develop resilience by facing challenges head-on, viewing setbacks as opportunities for growth, and cultivating a positive outlook.
- Emotional Control: Managing emotions effectively is crucial for maintaining focus and performing under pressure. Athletes learn to identify and regulate their emotions, using techniques like relax-

ation exercises, mindfulness practices, and positive self-talk.
- Focus and Concentration: Maintaining focus amidst distractions and pressure is essential for achieving peak performance. Athletes train their minds to concentrate on the present moment, eliminate negative thoughts, and stay laser-focused on their goals.
- Confidence and Self-Belief: A strong sense of self-belief is the cornerstone of mental toughness. Athletes cultivate confidence through visualization, positive affirmations, and celebrating their successes. This unwavering faith in their abilities fuels their performance and empowers them to overcome challenges.
- Adaptability and Flexibility: The ability to adapt to changing circumstances and embrace new challenges is crucial in today's dynamic workplace. Athletes develop adaptability by remaining open to new perspectives, embracing new challenges, and learning from their mistakes.

Strategies for Building Mental Toughness in Professionals:

1. Develop a Growth Mindset: Embrace the belief that your abilities are not fixed but can be developed through hard work and dedication. This mindset fosters resilience and motivates you to learn from setbacks.
2. Practice Mindfulness: Incorporate mindfulness practices like meditation and deep breathing into your daily routine. This helps manage stress, improve focus, and enhance emotional regulation.
3. Visualize Success: Regularly visualize yourself achieving your goals and performing at your best. This mental rehearsal boosts confidence and reinforces your belief in your abilities.
4. Cultivate Positive Self-Talk: Replace negative self-criticism with positive affirmations and self-encouragement. This fosters a positive mindset and empowers you to overcome challenges.

5. Build a Support Network: Surround yourself with positive and supportive individuals who believe in you and challenge you to grow. This network provides encouragement and guidance, especially during difficult times.

6. Embrace Challenges: View challenges and setbacks as opportunities for learning and growth. This mindset fosters resilience and motivates you to continually improve your skills and abilities.

7. Celebrate Achievements: Take the time to acknowledge and celebrate your accomplishments, no matter how small. This reinforces a positive self-image and boosts your confidence.

Remember: Building mental toughness is a continuous process, not a one-time achievement. By incorporating these strategies into your daily routine and consistently practicing them, you can cultivate the same mental fortitude as athletes and overcome any obstacle that arises in your career.

Actionable Tips:

- Start small and gradually increase the difficulty of your challenges.
- Reward yourself for sticking to your goals and celebrating your successes.
- Learn from your mistakes and use them to improve your performance.
- Seek professional help if you feel overwhelmed or struggle to manage stress.

When you approach your career with the unwavering mental toughness of an athlete, you become unstoppable. Remember, the challenges you face are not limitations but opportunities to grow and evolve. Embrace them with a positive mindset, and you will find yourself rising above any obstacle, achieving your goals, and ultimately reaching your full potential in the professional arena.

5

Embracing Collaboration and Teamwork: Building Winning Teams From the Court to the Conference Room

In the fast-paced world of sports, victory rarely comes at the hands of a single individual. It's through seamless teamwork, effective communication, and a shared vision that teams achieve greatness. This chapter delves into the collaborative spirit that drives athletic success and demonstrates how these same principles can be applied to create a thriving and productive work environment.

The Power of Collaboration:

- Synergy and Collective Intelligence: When individuals with diverse skillsets come together and work towards a common goal, the out-come is often greater than the sum of its parts. Athletes understand this principle intuitively, relying on the strengths and expertise of their teammates to achieve collective success.
- Enhanced Problem-Solving: Diverse perspectives lead to more creative and effective solutions. By collaborating, individuals

can challenge each other's assumptions and explore different approaches, leading to innovative solutions and breakthroughs.

- Improved Decision-Making: By leveraging the collective knowledge and experience of the team, leaders can make more informed and impactful decisions. Athletes rely on their coaches and teammates to analyze situations, provide feedback, and make adjustments as needed.
- Shared Responsibility and Support: Teamwork fosters a sense of shared responsibility and accountability, motivating individuals to perform their best. When team members know they are supported by their colleagues, they are more likely to take risks, overcome challenges, and achieve their goals.

Building a Collaborative Work Environment:

- Establish Clear Roles and Responsibilities: Define each team member's role and ensure everyone understands their individual responsibilities and how they contribute to the overall goals.
- Promote Open Communication: Encourage open dialogue and active listening within the team. Create a safe space where individuals feel comfortable sharing ideas, concerns, and feedback.
- Recognize and Celebrate Individual and Team Achievements: Acknowledge the contributions of each team member and celebrate both individual and team successes. This fosters a sense of belonging, appreciation, and motivates continued collaboration.
- Implement Effective Problem-Solving Strategies: Encourage brainstorming sessions, constructive feedback, and open discussions to explore different perspectives and find innovative solutions to challenges.
- Embrace Diversity and Inclusion: Cultivate a team environment that welcomes diverse perspectives, backgrounds, and experiences. This

fosters creativity, innovation, and a richer understanding of the challenges and opportunities faced by the organization.

Communication: The Lifeblood of Collaboration:

- Active Listening: Pay close attention to others, comprehend their viewpoints, and seek clarification if needed. Demonstrate a genuine interest in what your colleagues have to say.
- Clear and Concise Communication: Articulate your thoughts and ideas clearly and concisely, avoiding ambiguity and ensuring everyone is on the same page.
- Effective Feedback: Provide constructive feedback that is specific, actionable, and delivered respectfully. Use feedback to encourage learning and development within the team.
- Nonverbal Communication: Be mindful of your body language and tone of voice, as these can significantly impact the message you convey.
- Embrace Different Communication Styles: Recognize that individuals have different communication preferences and adapt your approach accordingly to ensure effective understanding and collaboration.

By adopting the collaborative spirit and communication skills honed by athletes, you can transform your workplace into a breeding ground for innovation, success, and individual fulfillment. Remember, teamwork is not a matter of individual talent; it's about leveraging the collective strengths and expertise of your team to achieve common goals and create a truly winning environment.

Actionable Tips:

- Organize team-building activities to foster trust and collaboration.
- Implement regular team meetings to discuss progress, challenges, and solutions.
- Utilize collaborative technology tools to facilitate communication and project management.
- Encourage cross-functional collaboration to break down silos and promote knowledge sharing.
- Conduct regular team surveys to assess communication effectiveness and identify areas for improvement.

When you approach your work with the same collaborative spirit and effective communication skills that drive athletic success, you will unlock the true potential of your team and achieve remarkable results in the workplace.

6

Leadership Through Action and Inspiration: From Locker Room Captains to Boardroom Visionaries

On the playing field, leaders emerge not just through titles but through their actions and ability to inspire their teammates. Similarly, in the professional arena, true leadership goes beyond positional authority. This chapter delves into the varied leadership styles observed in athletes and demonstrates how these styles can be harnessed to motivate, guide, and empower individuals and teams toward achieving their full potential.

Leadership Styles Observed in Athletes:

- The Captain: This leader is the embodiment of the team's values and spirit. They lead by example, demonstrating dedication, hard work, and unwavering commitment to their goals. Their actions inspire and motivate others, fostering a sense of unity and shared purpose.
- The Motivator: This leader possesses an infectious enthusiasm and optimism that uplifts and energizes the team. They offer encouragement and support, helping teammates overcome challenges and

maintain focus during difficult times.

- The Strategist: This leader has a keen eye for detail and excels at planning and execution. They analyze situations, assess risks, and formulate strategies to achieve desired outcomes. Their ability to anticipate challenges and adapt to changing situations guides the team toward success.
- The Tactician: This leader focuses on the practicalities of execution. They provide clear instructions, delegate tasks effectively, and hold teammates accountable for their contributions. Their focus on specific actions and efficient task management ensures smooth operation and optimal performance.
- The Visionary: This leader inspires the team with a bold vision for the future. They set ambitious goals, challenge the status quo, and motivate individuals to strive for greatness. Their ability to see the bigger picture and communicate it effectively fosters innovation and commitment within the team.

Translating Athletic Leadership Styles to the Workplace:

- Identify Your Leadership Style: Reflect on your strengths, weaknesses, and natural tendencies to identify which leadership style best aligns with your personality and values.
- Lead by Example: Just as athletes inspire their teammates through their actions, demonstrate your commitment to the team and its goals through your work ethic, dedication, and positive attitude.
- Motivate and Encourage: Foster a positive and supportive work environment by recognizing individual contributions, offering constructive feedback, and celebrating achievements.
- Develop Strategic Thinking: Analyze challenges, identify opportunities, and formulate clear plans to achieve desired outcomes. Adapt your strategies as needed to navigate changing circumstances and

keep the team on track.

- Delegate Effectively: Empower team members by delegating tasks that leverage their strengths. Provide clear instructions, offer guidance, and hold them accountable for their contributions.
- Inspire with a Shared Vision: Articulate a compelling vision for the future of your team or organization. Communicate this vision clearly and consistently, and motivate individuals to strive towards achieving it together.

Remember, leadership is not a one-size-fits-all proposition. Effective leaders adapt their style to the specific needs of their team and the situation at hand. By drawing inspiration from the diverse leadership styles observed in athletes, you can develop your unique leadership approach to motivate, guide, and inspire your team to achieve remarkable results.

Actionable Tips:

- Seek opportunities to observe and learn from different leadership styles.
- Mentor and empower individuals within your team to develop their leadership potential.
- Create a feedback loop to receive insights from your team and improve your leadership effectiveness.
- Be open to adapting your leadership style as needed to meet the changing needs of your team and organization.
- Lead with integrity and authenticity, demonstrating your genuine commitment to the team and its goals.

When you approach leadership with the same dedication, passion, and adaptability as athletes, you will inspire your team, navigate challenges effectively, and ultimately lead them toward achieving their full potential.

II

The Athlete's Toolkit: Strategies for Winning in Business

7

Communication and Feedback: The Play-by-Play of Collaboration

Communication and feedback are the lifeblood of any successful team. Just as athletes rely on clear communication and constructive feedback to coordinate their actions and achieve victory on the field, professionals must cultivate similar skills to navigate the complexities of the workplace and ensure project success. This chapter dives into the effective communication techniques learned by athletes and coaches, and demonstrates their impact on team dynamics and project outcomes.

Communication Techniques from the Playing Field:

- Clarity and Concision: Athletes are trained to communicate clearly and concisely, eliminating ambiguity and ensuring everyone is on the same page. This approach minimizes misunderstandings and fosters efficient collaboration.
- Active Listening: Effective communication goes beyond simply speaking. Athletes learn to actively listen, paying attention to verbal and non-verbal cues, and demonstrating genuine interest in what others are saying.

- Respectful Disagreement: Athletes understand that disagreement is a natural part of any collaborative process. They practice disagreeing respectfully, focusing on issues, not personalities, and seeking solutions that benefit the team.
- Positive Reinforcement: Coaches and players understand the power of positive reinforcement. They celebrate successes, acknowledge individual contributions, and offer constructive feedback to motivate and inspire each other.
- Open and Honest Feedback: Athletes are encouraged to provide and receive open and honest feedback. They learn to deliver feedback in a timely and respectful manner, focusing on specific behaviors and offering actionable suggestions for improvement.

Impact of Communication and Feedback on Team Dynamics:

- Increased Trust and Collaboration: Clear communication fosters trust among team members, creating an environment where individuals feel comfortable expressing their ideas and collaborating effectively.
- Reduced Conflict: By addressing issues directly and constructively, effective communication minimizes misunderstandings and resolves conflicts quickly, preventing them from escalating and impacting team performance.
- Enhanced Problem-Solving: When team members communicate openly and share diverse perspectives, they are better equipped to identify problems, brainstorm solutions, and arrive at effective decisions collaboratively.
- Improved Motivation and Engagement: Positive reinforcement and constructive feedback motivate individuals to perform at their best and feel valued for their contributions, leading to higher levels of engagement and commitment to the team's goals.

- Enhanced Project Success: Clear communication and effective feedback ensure everyone is aligned on project objectives, facilitates efficient execution, and enables the team to anticipate and address challenges before they derail progress.

Implementing Effective Communication and Feedback Practices:

- Establish clear communication channels and protocols.
- Hold regular team meetings and encourage open dialogue.
- Practice active listening and show genuine interest in others' perspectives.
- Provide and receive feedback in a timely, respectful, and constructive manner.
- Celebrate successes and acknowledge individual contributions.
- Use technology to facilitate communication and collaboration.

Remember, effective communication and feedback are not one-time events; they are ongoing processes that require ongoing effort and commitment from all team members. By adopting the communication techniques and feedback practices honed by athletes, you can cultivate a more collaborative, productive, and ultimately, successful team in the workplace.

Actionable Tips:

- Schedule regular one-on-one meetings to provide and receive feedback.
- Use role-playing exercises to practice providing and receiving difficult feedback.
- Implement a feedback loop to encourage continuous improvement.
- Seek feedback from mentors and colleagues to identify areas for

improvement.

- Model effective communication behaviors and encourage others to do the same.

By fostering a culture of open communication and constructive feedback, you can transform your team into a well-oiled machine, capable of tackling any challenge and achieving remarkable results.

8

Building Strong Relationships: The Team Spirit in Action

From the camaraderie of the locker room to the grit of the playing field, the success of any athletic team hinges on the strength of its relationships. Athletes cultivate trust, respect, and a shared sense of purpose to overcome challenges, achieve victory, and forge a lasting bond. This same team spirit, when translated to the workplace, can foster healthy and productive relationships, propelling individuals and teams toward remarkable achievements.

The Cornerstones of Strong Team Relationships:

- Trust and Respect: Athletes understand that trust and respect are the bedrock of effective collaboration. They build trust through their actions, demonstrating reliability, honesty, and accountability. Respect manifests in valuing diverse perspectives, treating colleagues with courtesy, and celebrating individual contributions.
- Open and Effective Communication: Clear communication and active listening form the foundation of understanding and trust. Athletes practice open and honest communication, providing con-

structive feedback, and creating a safe space for expressing ideas
and concerns without fear of judgment.

- Shared Vision and Goals: When individuals are united by a common
vision and a set of shared goals, it creates a powerful force driving
commitment and motivation. Athletes work towards these goals as a
united front, supporting and motivating each other, and celebrating
collective achievements.
- Empathy and Emotional Intelligence: Recognizing and acknowledg-
ing the emotions of others is crucial for building strong relationships.
Athletes develop empathy by observing their teammates' nonverbal
cues, offering support during difficult times, and celebrating their
successes with genuine enthusiasm.
- Shared Responsibility and Accountability: When individuals feel
responsible for their actions and the team's success, it fosters a
sense of ownership and commitment. Athletes hold themselves and
their teammates accountable, ensuring everyone contributes to the
best of their abilities.

Translating Athletic Relationships to the Workplace:

- Get to Know Your Colleagues: Invest time in understanding your
colleagues' interests, strengths, and challenges. This fosters con-
nection and builds bridges.
- Practice Active Listening: Pay close attention to what your colleagues are saying, both verbally and nonverbally, to fully grasp
their perspectives and concerns.
- Offer and Receive Feedback Constructively: Provide feedback in a
timely, respectful, and actionable manner. Be receptive to receiving
feedback yourself and use it to improve your relationships and
performance.
- Celebrate Successes Together: Take time to acknowledge and cele-

brate individual and team achievements. This strengthens the bond between colleagues and reinforces a sense of shared accomplishment.

- Offer Support and Encouragement: Be there for your colleagues during difficult times. Offer encouragement, assistance, and a listening ear, demonstrating genuine care and support.
- Be Reliable and Trustworthy: Meet your commitments, be honest in your communication, and demonstrate reliability. This builds trust and encourages others to rely on you.
- Show Respect for Diverse Perspectives: Value the opinions and experiences of your colleagues, even when they differ from your own. This fosters a more inclusive and collaborative work environment.
- Promote a Culture of Open Communication: Encourage open dialogue and create a safe space for individuals to express their ideas and concerns without fear of judgment. This fosters trust and allows for constructive problem-solving.

By cultivating the same values and practices that athletes use to build strong relationships on the field, you can foster a more collaborative, supportive, and ultimately, successful workplace. Remember, strong relationships are not built overnight; they require consistent effort, genuine interest in others, and a commitment to building a team spirit that extends far beyond the individual.

Actionable Tips:

- Organize team-building activities to encourage interaction and relationship-building.
- Implement regular team meetings to foster open communication and collaboration.
- Practice giving and receiving compliments regularly.

- Offer mentorship and support to colleagues seeking guidance or facing challenges.
- Recognize and celebrate individual and team achievements publicly.
- Utilize technology to stay connected and foster communication outside of the office.

When you prioritize building strong relationships in the workplace, you create a foundation for trust, collaboration, and ultimately, remarkable success. Remember, the team spirit that champions athletes to victory can also propel your career to new heights.

9

Conflict Resolution: Learning to Pivot and Play Fair

From heated exchanges on the court to passionate disagreements in the boardroom, conflict is an inevitable part of any competitive environment. While it can be disruptive and challenging, navigating conflict effectively can be the key to unlocking stronger relationships, improved collaboration, and ultimately, greater success. This chapter delves into the strategies athletes use to resolve conflict and demonstrates how these approaches can be applied to navigate workplace disagreements constructively.

Athletes' Approach to Conflict Resolution:

- Focus on the Issue, Not the Person: Athletes learn to separate the issue at hand from personal attacks. They focus on the specific problem and work towards finding a solution that benefits the team, avoiding blaming individuals or resorting to personal insults.
- Active Listening and Open Communication: Effective communication is crucial for resolving conflict. Athletes practice active listening, paying attention to their teammates' concerns and perspectives,

and communicating their own thoughts and feelings openly and honestly.

- Empathy and Understanding: Athletes recognize that conflict often arises from different perspectives and approaches. They strive to understand their teammates' viewpoints and consider their feelings, fostering empathy and a willingness to find common ground.

- Seeking Solutions through Collaboration: Rather than viewing conflict as a win-lose situation, athletes approach it as an opportunity to find a collaborative solution that benefits everyone involved. This fosters a sense of shared responsibility and ownership over the outcome.

- Maintaining Respect and Professionalism: Even in the midst of disagreement, athletes maintain respect for their teammates and colleagues. They avoid resorting to unprofessional behavior or harmful communication, ensuring the conflict remains focused on finding a resolution.

Applying Athletic Strategies to Workplace Conflict:

- Identify the Core Issue: Clearly define the root cause of the conflict. This helps focus the discussion and avoid getting bogged down in irrelevant details or personal attacks.

- Listen Actively and Seek Clarification: Give your colleagues your full attention and actively listen to their perspectives. Ask clarifying questions to ensure you fully understand their concerns.

- Express Your Concerns Clearly and Respectfully: Communicate your own position calmly and respectfully, focusing on the issue and avoiding personal attacks.

- Compromise and Find Common Ground: Be willing to compromise and find solutions that address the needs and concerns of all parties involved.

- Focus on Solutions and Collaborative Outcomes: Work together with your colleagues to identify solutions that benefit everyone and contribute to a positive outcome for the team or organization.
- Maintain Professionalism and Respect: Throughout the conflict resolution process, uphold professional standards and treat others with respect, even when you disagree.

Additional Tips for Effective Conflict Resolution:

- Seek mediation or intervention from a neutral third party if needed.
- Take a break and cool down if tempers are running high.
- Focus on the future and how to move forward constructively.
- Learn from the experience and seek ways to prevent similar conflicts from arising in the future.

Remember, conflict is not inherently negative; it can be an opportunity for growth and improvement. By applying the strategies used by athletes, you can approach workplace disagreements with confidence, navigate them constructively, and ultimately foster stronger relationships and achieve greater success.

Actionable Tips:

- Practice active listening skills and role-play conflict resolution scenarios with colleagues.
- Attend training programs or workshops on conflict resolution and communication skills.
- Develop a personal toolkit of strategies for managing emotions and de-escalating tense situations.
- Implement conflict resolution protocols within your team or organization.

- Seek feedback from colleagues and mentors on your approach to conflict resolution.

By actively honing your conflict resolution skills and adopting the same sportsmanship and collaborative spirit as athletes, you can turn conflict into a catalyst for positive change and achieve remarkable results in your professional endeavors.

10

Adaptability and Quick Thinking: Scoring Points with Change

From unexpected injuries to last-minute game-changing plays, the world of sports is a constant reminder that the only certainty is change. Athletes cultivate the remarkable ability to adapt to these unforeseen circumstances, respond with quick thinking, and seize new opportunities to emerge victorious. This chapter delves into the secrets of athletic adaptability and demonstrates how these skills can be harnessed by professionals to navigate the ever-shifting landscape of the modern workplace.

The Power of Adaptability in Athletics:

- Anticipating Change: Successful athletes anticipate potential challenges and formulate contingency plans. They analyze opponents, assess their own strengths and weaknesses, and develop strategies for adapting to different scenarios.
- Reacting with Speed and Decisiveness: When faced with unexpected situations, athletes react quickly and decisively, drawing upon their instincts, training, and experience to make informed choices in real-

time.

- Maintaining Focus and Composure: Adaptability thrives amidst pressure. Athletes learn to maintain focus and composure in the face of change, avoiding distractions and remaining calm under pressure to make sound decisions.
- Embracing Opportunities for Growth: Adaptability is not about simply surviving change; it's about thriving through it. Athletes view change as an opportunity to learn, grow, and develop new skills, expanding their capabilities and adapting to the evolving demands of their sport.

Adapting Athletic Skills to the Workplace:

- Embrace a Growth Mindset: View change not as a threat, but as an opportunity for learning and growth. Cultivate a curious and open-minded attitude, and seek out new challenges to expand your skillset.
- Develop Strong Analytical Skills: Regularly assess your strengths, weaknesses, and the changing environment around you. This allows you to anticipate potential challenges and prepare for a range of scenarios.
- Practice Quick Decision-Making: Develop your ability to think on your feet and make informed decisions quickly. Utilize simulations, role-playing exercises, and critical thinking games to hone this skill.
- Maintain a Calm and Composed Demeanor: Even in the face of unexpected challenges, strive to remain calm and collected. Practice stress management techniques and develop strategies for maintaining focus under pressure.
- Collaborate and Share Knowledge: Adapting is easier with a team. Actively seek input from colleagues, share knowledge, and work collaboratively to develop innovative solutions to challenges.

- Be Open to Feedback and Continuous Improvement: Regularly solicit feedback from colleagues and mentors to identify areas for improvement. Be open to learning from your mistakes and continually strive to adapt and refine your skills.

Remember, the ability to adapt and think quickly is not a fixed trait; it is a skill that can be honed and developed through practice and dedication. By adopting the same mindset and strategies as athletes, you can unlock greater adaptability in your professional life, navigate change with confidence, and achieve remarkable results.

Actionable Tips:

- Engage in scenario planning exercises to prepare for potential changes in your industry or organization.
- Seek opportunities to learn new skills and broaden your knowledge base.
- Challenge yourself with tasks that lie outside your comfort zone.
- Practice mindfulness and meditation techniques to improve your focus and clarity under pressure.
- Network with colleagues and professionals from diverse backgrounds to expand your perspective.
- Actively seek feedback and opportunities for continuous learning and development.

When you embrace adaptability and quick thinking as hallmarks of your professional identity, you become a valuable asset in any dynamic work environment, capable of meeting challenges head-on, seizing opportunities, and achieving remarkable success.

11

Taking Initiative and Owning Your Position: Leading from the Front

From the captain on the court to the rookie striving to prove themselves, athletes share a common trait: the unwavering commitment to taking ownership and responsibility for their performance. This dedication to personal accountability fuels athletic excellence and fosters a culture of collaboration and success within the team. In the professional arena, cultivating this same mindset can unlock unparalleled growth, propel career advancement, and establish you as a leader in your field.

The Athlete's Mindset of Ownership:

- Individual Accountability: Athletes understand that their individual performance directly impacts the team's success. They hold themselves accountable for their actions, consistently strive to improve, and take full responsibility for their results.
- Proactive Approach: Athletes don't wait to be told what to do. They anticipate needs, proactively seek out opportunities to contribute, and take initiative in tackling challenges and finding solutions.
- Embracing Responsibility: Athletes take ownership of their mis-

takes, learn from them, and use them as opportunities for growth. They don't shy away from responsibility, but view it as an essential stepping stone to achieving their full potential.

- Continuously Learning and Improving: Athletes are dedicated to lifelong learning and continuous improvement. They actively seek feedback, embrace new challenges, and invest in acquiring the skills and knowledge necessary to excel in their field.
- Leading by Example: Athletes set a positive example for their teammates through their dedication, commitment, and self-accountability. They inspire and motivate others to strive for excellence and contribute their best efforts towards achieving shared goals.

Harnessing the Power of Ownership in the Workplace:

- Define Your Goals and Objectives: Clearly define your personal and professional goals. This provides a roadmap for your efforts and helps you identify areas where you need to take ownership.
- Proactively Seek Opportunities: Don't wait for opportunities to be handed to you. Actively seek out projects, challenges, and tasks that allow you to expand your skillset, gain new experiences, and contribute to your team's success.
- Take Initiative and Be a Problem Solver: Don't wait for instructions. Identify problems, propose solutions, and take initiative to implement them. This demonstrates your leadership potential and ability to take ownership of your work.
- Seek Feedback and Embrace Continuous Improvement: Actively solicit feedback from colleagues and mentors to identify areas for improvement. Embrace constructive criticism and use it as a catalyst for growth and development.
- Hold Yourself Accountable: Take full responsibility for your actions,

both successes and failures. Learn from your mistakes and use them as opportunities to improve and refine your skills.

- Communicate Effectively and Collaboratively: Clearly communicate your goals, progress, and challenges to your colleagues and superiors. Collaborate effectively with others and share ownership of projects and objectives.

Remember, taking initiative and owning your position is not a one-time act; it's a continuous commitment to personal growth and professional development. By adopting the same mindset as athletes, you can unlock your full potential, become a valuable asset to your organization, and pave the way for a successful and fulfilling career.

Actionable Tips:

- Set SMART goals for yourself and regularly track your progress.
- Volunteer for challenging tasks and projects.
- Identify and address problems before they escalate.
- Seek mentorship and actively learn from experienced professionals.
- Take ownership of your mistakes and develop a plan for improvement.
- Communicate openly and honestly with your colleagues and superiors.
- Share your knowledge and expertise with others.

By embracing the athlete's mindset of ownership and taking initiative in your professional life, you transform into a self-directed, empowered individual capable of achieving remarkable success and propelling yourself towards your career goals.

III

Achieving Peak Performance: Maintaining Your Competitive Edge

12

Maintaining Motivation and Drive: The Long Game of Your Career

The journey of a successful career, like the path of an athlete, is a marathon, not a sprint. It requires unwavering motivation, unwavering commitment, and the ability to overcome setbacks and challenges. Athletes possess a unique ability to maintain their drive and passion throughout their demanding careers, and this chapter delves into their secrets, demonstrating how professionals can apply these strategies to stay motivated and engaged in the workplace.

The Athlete's Blueprint for Sustained Motivation:

- Passion and Purpose: Athletes are driven by a deep passion for their sport and a clear sense of purpose. They connect their everyday actions to their long-term goals, ensuring their efforts are meaningful and fulfilling.
- Setting SMART Goals: Athletes set specific, measurable, achievable, relevant, and time-bound goals. This framework provides a roadmap for their progress, keeps them focused, and offers milestones to celebrate along the way.

- Visualizing Success: Athletes leverage the power of visualization to see themselves achieving their goals. This visualization reinforces their commitment, boosts their confidence, and fuels their motivation.
- Embracing Challenges and Setbacks: Athletes view challenges and setbacks as opportunities for growth. They learn from their mistakes, adapt their strategies, and become even more resilient in the face of adversity.
- Celebrating Successes: Athletes take time to acknowledge and celebrate their achievements, no matter how small. This reinforces positive behavior, boosts morale, and motivates them to continue striving for excellence.
- Maintaining a Growth Mindset: Athletes believe in their ability to learn and grow. They embrace new challenges and view them as opportunities to expand their skills and knowledge.
- Finding Balance and Avoiding Burnout: Athletes understand the importance of maintaining a healthy work-life balance. They engage in activities outside their sport to prevent burnout and recharge their batteries.

Boosting Motivation in the Workplace:

- Identify Your Passions and Values: Reflect on what motivates you and align your career with your passions and values. This leads to greater fulfillment and sustained engagement in your work.
- Set Clear and Compelling Goals: Define your personal and professional goals using the SMART framework. This provides direction, focus, and a sense of progress towards achieving your aspirations.
- Visualize Your Success: Take time to visualize yourself accomplishing your goals. This mental exercise reinforces your commitment, builds your confidence, and fuels your motivation.

- Embrace Challenges as Opportunities: View challenges and setbacks as learning experiences. Analyze your mistakes, adapt your strategies, and use them as stepping stones to reach your full potential.
- Celebrate Achievements, Big and Small: Recognize and celebrate your successes, regardless of their magnitude. This reinforces positive behavior and motivates you to maintain your efforts.
- Develop a Growth Mindset: Believe in your ability to learn and grow. Embrace new challenges and opportunities as avenues for expanding your skillset and knowledge.
- Maintain a Healthy Work-Life Balance: Prioritize activities outside of work to avoid burnout. Engage in hobbies, spend time with loved ones, and recharge your batteries to maintain your energy and enthusiasm.

Remember, maintaining motivation is not a passive endeavor; it requires consistent effort and a proactive approach. By adopting the strategies used by athletes, you can cultivate a resilient mindset, reignite your passion, and embark on a fulfilling career journey.

Actionable Tips:

- Create a vision board that visualizes your career goals.
- Read inspirational stories of successful individuals.
- Join professional organizations and attend industry events.
- Develop a network of mentors and colleagues who support your goals.
- Regularly reflect on your progress and make adjustments as needed.
- Engage in activities that bring you joy and rejuvenation.
- Seek professional help if you experience burnout or demotivation.

By adopting the athlete's approach to motivation and integrating these strategies into your professional life, you can transform into a driven and passionate individual, capable of navigating the long game of your career with unwavering commitment and achieving remarkable success.

13

Continuous Learning and Skill Development: The Ongoing Training Regimen

In the ever-evolving landscape of professional life, staying ahead of the curve requires a commitment to continuous learning and skill development. Just as athletes dedicate themselves to rigorous training regimens to maintain their competitive edge, professionals must adopt a similar approach to upskill and adapt to the changing demands of their industries. This chapter delves into the strategies athletes use to consistently improve their abilities and demonstrates how these practices can be applied by professionals to accelerate their career growth and achieve remarkable success.

The Athlete's Approach to Continuous Learning:

- Seeking Out Feedback: Athletes actively seek feedback from coaches, mentors, and teammates to identify areas for improvement. They embrace constructive criticism and use it as a blueprint for refining their skills.
- Setting Learning Goals: Athletes set specific learning goals aligned with their overall career aspirations. This provides a clear roadmap

for their progress and ensures their efforts are targeted and impactful.

- Engaging in Deliberate Practice: Athletes practice with purpose and focus, pushing themselves outside their comfort zones to refine their skills and develop new ones. They utilize various training methods to maximize their learning and performance.

- Embracing Continuous Growth Mindset: Athletes believe in their ability to learn and improve throughout their careers. They approach challenges as opportunities for growth and view setbacks as stepping stones towards achieving their full potential.

- Seeking Diverse Learning Opportunities: Athletes diversify their learning by attending workshops, conferences, and seminars. They actively engage in professional development activities and explore new resources to stay ahead of the curve.

- Mentorship and Collaborative Learning: Athletes seek guidance and mentorship from experienced professionals. They value collabora- tive learning and actively share knowledge and expertise with their peers.

Implementing the Athlete's Learning Model in the Workplace:

- Seek Regular Feedback and Performance Reviews: Actively solicit feedback from colleagues, mentors, and superiors. Utilize this feedback to identify areas for improvement and create a personalized development plan.

- Set SMART Learning Goals: Define specific, measurable, achievable, relevant, and time-bound goals for your skill development. This provides a clear path for your learning journey and ensures your efforts are focused and effective.

- Practice Deliberately: Utilize various learning methods, such as online courses, workshops, and one-on-one coaching, to acquire new skills and refine existing ones. Practice consistently and push yourself beyond your comfort zone to maximize your learning.

- Develop a Growth Mindset: Cultivate a belief in your ability to learn and grow throughout your career. Embrace challenges as opportunities to expand your knowledge and develop new skills.
- Pursue Diverse Learning Opportunities: Attend industry events, webinars, and conferences to stay abreast of the latest trends and best practices in your field. Explore online learning platforms and educational resources to acquire new knowledge.
- Connect with Mentors and Collaborate with Peers: Seek guidance from experienced professionals and actively participate in professional communities. Share your knowledge and expertise with colleagues to foster a collaborative learning environment.

Remember, continuous learning and skill development are not optional; they are essential for navigating the dynamic and competitive professional landscape. By applying the same strategies used by athletes, you can transform into a lifelong learner, cultivate a resilient and adaptable mindset, and stay ahead of the curve in your career journey.

Actionable Tips:

- Create a personalized learning plan and track your progress against your goals.
- Identify and connect with mentors who can provide guidance and support.
- Join professional organizations and online communities to stay connected with your peers.
- Allocate time in your schedule for learning and development activities.
- Experiment with different learning methods to find what works best

for you.
- Read industry publications and blogs to stay updated on the latest trends.
- Share your knowledge and expertise with others through presentations, workshops, or online courses.

By integrating the athlete's spirit of continuous learning into your professional life, you become an agile and adaptable professional who is capable of thriving in the ever-evolving world of work and achieving remarkable success.

14

Building a Winning Support System: The Team Behind You

In the relentless pursuit of professional success, few achieve remarkable feats alone. Just as athletes rely on their coaches, teammates, and trainers to achieve victory, professionals require a strong support system of mentors, colleagues, and friends to navigate the challenges and opportunities they encounter on their career journeys. This chapter delves into the importance of building a winning support system, exploring how these individuals can contribute to your growth and propel you toward achieving your goals.

The Power of a Supportive Network:

- Mentorship and Guidance: Mentors offer invaluable wisdom, experience, and guidance. They provide constructive feedback, challenge your assumptions, and help you navigate career transitions and challenges.
- Collaboration and Learning: A supportive network of colleagues fosters collaboration and learning. You share knowledge, expertise, and resources, enriching your understanding and accelerating your

professional development.

- Emotional Support and Encouragement: During challenging times, a strong network provides emotional support and encouragement. They offer a listening ear, celebrate your successes, and help you navigate setbacks with resilience.
- Expanding Your Horizons and Opportunities: Your network can connect you with new opportunities, introduce you to key individuals, and open doors to career advancement. They act as your advocates and champions, helping you showcase your talents and achieve your full potential.
- Building a Sense of Belonging: A supportive network creates a sense of belonging and community. You connect with individuals who share your values and aspirations, fostering a sense of belonging and reducing feelings of isolation.

Building Your Winning Team:

- Identify Potential Mentors: Look to experienced professionals in your field or individuals who inspire you. Seek connections through professional organizations, networking events, or online platforms.
- Nurture Relationships and Invest Time: Building a strong network requires consistent effort. Invest time in fostering meaningful relationships with your mentors, colleagues, and friends.
- Be a Valuable Member of the Network: Offer your own expertise and support to others. Contribute to the network by sharing resources, offering guidance, and celebrating the successes of your peers.
- Be Open to Diverse Perspectives: Value the different perspectives and experiences within your network. This broadens your understanding and helps you approach challenges with greater insight.
- Maintain Open Communication and Transparency: Foster open and honest communication with your network. Share your goals,

challenges, and anxieties, and be receptive to their feedback and support.

· Express Gratitude and Appreciation: Acknowledge the contributions of your mentors, colleagues, and friends. Express your gratitude for their support and encouragement.

Remember, a winning support system is not built overnight; it requires continuous effort and a commitment to nurturing meaningful relationships. By actively seeking out mentors, fostering collaboration with colleagues, and building a network of individuals who share your values, you create a powerful foundation for achieving your career aspirations and reaching your full potential.

Actionable Tips:

· Attend industry events and conferences to expand your network.
· Join professional organizations and online communities related to your field.
· Reach out to potential mentors and express your interest in their guidance.
· Offer your expertise and support to other members of your network.
· Organize regular meetings or coffee chats with your mentors and colleagues.
· Utilize online platforms such as LinkedIn to connect with professionals.
· Participate in volunteer opportunities to meet individuals with diverse backgrounds.

By embracing the importance of a strong support system and proactively building your own winning team, you equip yourself with the resources, guidance, and encouragement necessary to navigate the challenges of your career journey and achieve remarkable success.

15

Maintaining Balance and Well-being: The Importance of Time Out

No matter how dedicated and passionate we are about our careers, pushing ourselves relentlessly without prioritizing well-being is a recipe for burnout and ultimately hinders our long-term success. Just as athletes understand the importance of rest and recovery for optimal performance, professionals must actively cultivate a healthy work-life balance and engage in self-care practices to ensure their energy, mental health, and overall well-being remain in peak condition.

Athletes' Approach to Balance and Well-being:

- Prioritizing Rest and Recovery: Athletes schedule adequate rest periods into their training regimens to allow their bodies to recover and rebuild. They understand that rest is not a luxury, but a necessity for peak performance.
- Maintaining a Healthy Lifestyle: Athletes prioritize healthy eating, regular exercise, and sufficient sleep to fuel their bodies and minds. They recognize that a healthy lifestyle is essential for optimal performance and long-term well-being.

- Engaging in Activities They Enjoy: Athletes dedicate time to activities outside their sport that bring them joy and relaxation. This helps them manage stress, reduce burnout, and maintain a sense of balance in their lives.
- Setting Boundaries and Saying No: Athletes learn to set healthy boundaries between their work and personal lives. They say no to excessive commitments and prioritize activities that contribute to their well-being.
- Seeking Support and Mental Health Resources: Athletes recognize the importance of mental health and emotional well-being. They seek professional support when needed and utilize resources to manage stress and anxiety.

Applying Athletic Practices to Professional Life:

- Schedule Time for Rest and Recovery: Regularly schedule time for rest and relaxation into your calendar. Disconnect from work, engage in activities you enjoy, and prioritize getting enough sleep.
- Maintain a Healthy Lifestyle: Prioritize healthy eating, regular exercise, and sufficient sleep. These practices improve your energy levels, focus, and overall well-being.
- Identify and Engage in Enjoyable Activities: Make time for activities outside of work that bring you pleasure and relaxation. This could include hobbies, spending time with loved ones, or pursuing creative endeavors.
- Set Boundaries and Manage Your Schedule: Learn to set healthy boundaries between your work and personal lives. Decline unreasonable demands and delegate tasks when needed.
- Prioritize Your Mental Health: Recognize the importance of mental health and actively manage stress and anxiety. Seek professional support when needed and utilize resources such as mindfulness

exercises, therapy, or meditation.

Remember, maintaining work-life balance and engaging in self-care are not signs of weakness; they are essential for long-term success and fulfillment. By adopting the same strategies as athletes, you can become a more resilient, productive, and successful professional, capable of achieving your goals without sacrificing your well-being.

Actionable Tips:

- Create a daily schedule that includes time for work, leisure, and self-care.
- Practice mindfulness exercises and meditation to manage stress and anxiety.
- Disconnect from work emails and notifications during your personal time.
- Delegate tasks and say no to commitments that overload your schedule.
- Regularly engage in activities that bring you joy and relaxation.
- Seek professional help if you experience burnout or mental health challenges.

By prioritizing well-being and integrating these practices into your professional life, you create a sustainable foundation for success, allowing you to perform at your best and achieve remarkable results while maintaining a healthy and balanced life.

16

The Lasting Impact of Athletic Values

The competitive arena of sports transcends the mere pursuit of victory; it serves as a crucible for forging character, instilling values, and equipping individuals with invaluable life lessons that extend far beyond the final score. This chapter delves into the enduring impact of athletic values, exploring how the lessons learned on the field and court continue to shape personal and professional growth throughout life.

The Legacy of Athletic Values:

- Discipline and Hard Work: Athletic pursuits demand unwavering discipline and consistent hard work. Through dedication and per-severance, athletes learn to push their limits, overcome challenges, and achieve their goals. This instilled discipline translates into all aspects of life, fostering a strong work ethic and a commitment to excellence.
- Resilience and Mental Toughness: Sports expose athletes to adver-sity and setbacks. They learn to overcome their failures, bounce back from setbacks, and develop mental toughness. This resilience equips them to navigate challenges, adapt to change, and persevere

in the face of difficulties, both on and off the field or court.

- Teamwork and Collaboration: Sports are inherently collaborative endeavors. Athletes learn to work together towards a common goal, communicate effectively, and rely on their teammates for support and success. These teamwork skills translate seamlessly into the workplace, fostering collaboration, communication, and a sense of shared responsibility.
- Sportsmanship and Respect: Winning and losing are integral parts of sports, but it is through sportsmanship and respect that true character is revealed. Athletes learn to play with integrity, respect their opponents, and handle both success and failure with grace. These values extend to all aspects of life, promoting ethical behavior, fair play, and respect for others.
- Leadership and Self-awareness: Sports offer opportunities for individuals to develop leadership skills and cultivate self-awareness. Athletes learn to motivate and inspire others, delegate tasks, and take responsibility for their actions. This self-awareness allows them to identify their strengths and weaknesses, set goals, and make informed decisions.

The Enduring Influence of Sports:

- Building a Positive Mindset: The lessons learned through sports foster a positive mindset. Athletes develop an optimistic outlook, a belief in their own abilities, and a willingness to take calculated risks. This positive attitude translates into all aspects of life, enhancing personal fulfillment and promoting professional success.
- Developing Lifelong Habits: The values instilled through sports become ingrained habits that shape an individual's life. Discipline, dedication, and collaboration become core principles, guiding decision-making and driving personal and professional growth.

- Creating a Foundation for Success: The lessons learned through sports provide a solid foundation for success in all aspects of life. Athletes develop the skills, values, and mindset necessary to navigate challenges, overcome obstacles, and achieve their goals, both on and off the field.
- Building Strong Relationships: Sports create a sense of community and belonging. The bonds forged through shared experiences, challenges, and victories last a lifetime. These strong relationships provide support, encouragement, and a sense of belonging, enriching personal and professional lives.
- Inspiring Others and Giving Back: The journey of an athlete can inspire others and leave a lasting impact on the world. Athletes have the opportunity to use their platform to advocate for positive change, mentor younger generations, and give back to their communities.

17

Conclusion: Embracing Your Winning Potential

As you turn the final page of this guide, remember the powerful athlete within you. You have the tools and the mindset to excel in the workplace, just as you did on the field or court. You possess the resilience to bounce back from setbacks, the adaptability to thrive in changing environments, and the leadership skills to inspire your colleagues.

Harness the power of your athletic past to fuel your professional future. Apply the lessons learned – the importance of teamwork, communication, self-discipline, and a relentless pursuit of excellence – to every challenge and opportunity that comes your way. Remember, every victory begins with a commitment to continuous learning and a belief in your own abilities.

Surround yourself with teammates who share your passion and support you on your journey. Embrace mentors who offer guidance and challenge you to reach your full potential. Prioritize your well-being, for a healthy mind and body are essential for sustained success.

Today, you stand on the threshold of a new game, one with its own set of rules and challenges. But the skills you honed as an athlete – the dedication, the focus, the unwavering spirit – are your greatest assets. With them in hand, you are ready to step onto the field and compete at the highest level.

So go forth, with confidence and conviction. Apply the lessons learned from this guide and embark on your own winning journey in the workplace. Remember, your journey doesn't end with the final whistle; it continues in the workplace, where every challenge is a new game to conquer. Apply these lessons, leverage your sports skills, and not only thrive but dominate in your professional arena.

Thank you for joining this journey. May your career be a testament to the triumphs of the game and the unwavering spirit of the athlete within you. Onward to victory!

18

Call to Action: Share Your Winning Story!

Did "Winning Strategies for Life: The Athlete's Guide to Thriving in the Workplace" inspire you to unlock your inner champion and achieve success in the workplace? Did the book offer valuable insights and practical strategies to help you navigate the challenges and opportunities of your career?

If so, we encourage you to share your experience with others by leaving a positive review on Amazon. Your review helps us reach a wider audience and empower more individuals to harness the athlete's spirit within them to achieve their professional goals.

Here are some ways you can help us spread the word:

- Leave a review on Amazon: Share your thoughts on the book's content, its impact on your career, and any specific lessons that resonated with you.
- Rate the book: Give "Winning Strategies for Life: The Athlete's Guide to Thriving in the Workplace" a 5-star rating to increase its visibility and encourage others to check it out.

- Share your review on social media: Let your network know about the book and encourage them to read it by sharing your review on platforms like Facebook, LinkedIn, and Twitter.

By taking these simple steps, you can help others discover the powerful lessons of "Winning Strategies for Life" and embark on their winning journeys in the workplace.

Thank you for being a part of our community and for your support!

About the Author

Susan Pierre-Louis is a lifelong athlete and a passionate advocate for applying the lessons learned on the court to success in all aspects of life. As a competitive volleyball player, she has firsthand experience in the power of teamwork, dedication, and a growth mindset. This experience, combined with her extensive career as a product manager, has led her to develop a unique perspective on the intersection of sports and professional success.

In her professional life, Susan applies the principles outlined in "Winning Strategies for Life: The Athlete's Guide to Thriving in the Workplace" to her work and strives to foster a collaborative and supportive environment for the teams she works with. This approach has earned her recognition as a leader, including several "Product Manager of the Year" awards. Her leadership style emphasizes recognizing and leveraging the strengths of each team member, creating a dynamic and high-performing environment.

Driven by a desire to empower others to achieve their full potential, Susan wrote "Winning Strategies for Life: The Athlete's Guide to Thriving in the Workplace" as a guide for athletes transitioning to the professional world and seasoned professionals seeking to reignite their passion and drive. She believes that the skills and values cultivated through sports are invaluable assets in the workplace and can be applied by anyone who seeks to achieve remarkable things in their career journey.

When not on the court or working, Susan enjoys spending time with her family and friends, exploring the outdoors, and engaging in activities that promote physical and mental well-being. She continues to be an avid learner, constantly seeking new ways to improve her skills and knowledge, both on and off the court.